Random Thoughts that make Sense.

ISBN: 979-8-9908056-2-0
(paperback)

First paperback edition July 2024
Book design by douzWriter

First printing edition 2024

About the Author

The author has been writing from a very young age, through elementary, high school, college and beyond. He has edited school and private papers, even at the doctoral level. One of his professors in college called him a "word smith" because of his unique style of writing. He has been a favorite of his professors of English composition, grammar and critical writing at every level of academic endeavor.

The writer has gone through the so called "university of hard knocks" in his life experiences. He is very much in tune with current affairs. He is a creature of conscience. He subscribes to fairness, and equal justice. Morally and spiritually, he is conservative. He is very liberal in the vein of kindness to others and is respectful of their environments, even where he disagrees with people.

He loves people. He loves to read and keep abreast of current issues, be it religious, socio-political, academic or in the area of public health. His interests are quite varied: he played for a few local soccer teams in Maryland and Virgina. He captained two of those teams as an attacking midfielder. Later in life, he successfully coached elementary and High School 'boys' and 'girls' soccer teams. All of these, as well as professional education, bring to bear on his general out look in life.

douz Writer

Preface

The articles in this book have been inspired by the experiences of the author, current events, reading, and studying, while drawing inferences therefrom, and getting inspiration for deep thoughts and pondering over old and new ideas.

How did I come up with these articles and thoughts and how would you, the reader, find the subjects and thoughts expressed in these pages, useful to you?

Here's the background: when I was in Elementary and High Schools, I used to read every copy of The Reader's Digest and Student Companion that I could lay my hands on. In Reader's Digest, I particularly enjoyed and imbibed the section on "Quotable Quotes". Those were stories and thoughts I pondered over, even, as I grew older. Quotable Quotes made me think critically, not just for what the words meant, but "Quotes" provided me with deep thoughts and ideas contained therein. They made me think deeper than I would have ordinarily. I later find myself using some of those quotes when I write or speak in public.

I was also influenced by debate contents, and current affairs. I learned from the afore mentioned Student Companion, and was drawn to the section on "Comparisons". A few of these expressions still ring in my mind: such phrases like "as dead as a door nail", "as sure as death and taxes", "as tall as a giant", "as deep as the sea", and "as high as the heavens", to recall a few.

It is our sincere hope that our readers will enjoy this book, be inspired by what you read, and draw inspiration and deep thinking from each article.

We believe that you, our readers, can use some of our content to enhance your speeches, or illustrate your messages with thoughts and ideas as those from "Quotable Quotes", "Student Companion", and as current affairs have helped to shape my own thoughts. Along with some scriptural passages.

May God richly bless you .

Contents

i About the Author

II Preface

1   Rebel, do You have a Cause? 1

2   Giving Advice   5

3   Faith in Action   10

4   Prayer and Miracles   16

5   Power of Prayer   22

6   Love as God Loves   26

7   Don't Stay Fallen   29

8   The Gold in Humans   35

9   Action Compliments Faith   45

10 The Bane of Self   48

11 Team   54

12 I Can't   58

13 Just Think   61

14 It is All About You   64

15 Empathy   70

16 Scriptural Quotes to "Ponder" 74

17 Prayer   80

1
Rebel, do You have a Cause?

Really, What are You Angry About?

Take a look at this picture. What do you see? What do you think or deduce from it?

Think it through:

Is a little "quib" worth a life of separation and the lack of communication and sharing with one another?

Why do we spend so much time being angry, even after we forget the real reason we got angry in the first place? Why do we keep quarreling unnecessarily and endlessly! Is this not the real definition of being a "rebel without a cause"?

Why are you angry for this long? Why are you fighting for this long? If you cannot answer these questions sincerely and clearly, it is time to seek peace or just live peacefully.

Our inner selves call us to choose peace and progress, rather than war and chaos.

"Come now, and let us reason together, saith the Lord: though your sins be as scarlet, they shall be as white as snow; though they be red like crimson, they shall be as wool". Isaiah 1:18

Talk things over, especially where you feel offended. You definitely can overcome disagreements and avoid unnecessary fights.

2
Giving Advice

Before you counsel or advise anyone, heed this:

.

2 Tim 4:2   .
"... exhort with all long suffering and doctrine".

"preach the word; be instant in season, and out of season, reprove, rebuke, exhort, with all long suffering and doctrine".

This is a season for advice and counter advice in our body politic, even, in our daily lives. We find ourselves in situations where we are called to give advice or receive the same. Many tend to jump to premature conclusions or become eager talkers instead of thinking things through before they advise those who baldly need wise counsel and guidance.

Before we give any admonition, whether in a home, civic or professional settings, or when people preach, the Apostle Paul admonishes us to be proper as to timeliness and the appropriateness of our counsel. We all ought to be willing to speak power to truth: rebuke if we have to, praise or affirm the individual(s) if we need to do so, with patience and candor.

_____   _____

In whatever endeavor or pursuit, we ought to prepare ourselves- such as being well informed on the issues involved, so that our advice is not just empty and drawn out talks.

We can take it from the secular world that states: "he that thinketh by the inch, but talketh by the yard, needeth to be kicketh by the foot". This is not a biblical quote, but it makes sense. doesn't it! It makes me believe that a good counselor must allow himself or herself to invest the

time to be well informed, to be sincere,as well as talk less and listen more. "Nuf Said"!
May God bless your days with wisdom, honesty and patience, as you counsel those who need your advice!

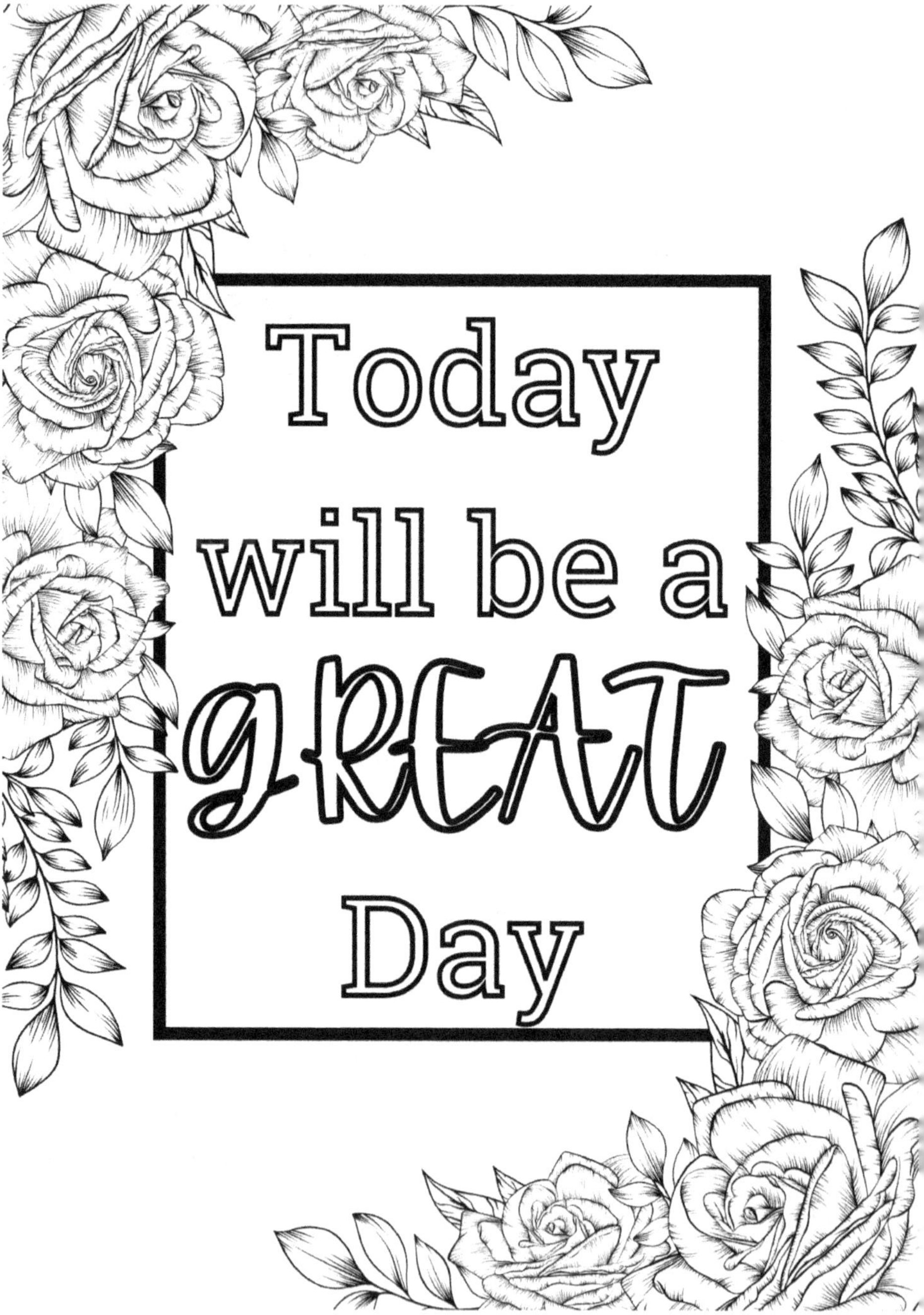
Today
will be a
GREAT
Day

3
Faith in Action

Faith in Action

Hebrews 11:1

Now, faith is the assurance of things hoped for, the conviction of things not seen.

From Matthew 21:21, Jesus Christ states, "Truly I tell you, if you have faith and do not doubt, not only can you curse the fruitless fig tree of the Bible, but also you can say to this mountain, 'Go, throw yourself into the sea,' and it will be done. Wow! How would you have felt in the shoes of the very old man, father Abraham!

FAITH IN ACTION

Could you imagine being in the shoes of the widow of Zarephath! You have only the last bit of oil and flour- just enough to make one last, one course of meal for your son and you to eat, after which you would starve to death, Then this stranger comes in and asks you to fix that meal for him, and him only. You are staring death in the face and Elijah dares ask for your very last available meal for himself only! Won't you just chase him away? You would, won't you! But with abundant faith in God, you would oblige. As the case here is, it turned out that with God's blessings, her family always had more than enough to eat every day after this experience in selflessness and deep faith.

Yes, God rewards our simple acts of faith mightily. In these days of uncertainty in our lives, where people are hungry, very hungry, lacking in funds, and food and threatened by uncertainty as to life and health, are you willing to give all you have in order to help others that need your help?

Put yourself in father Abraham's shoes, ready to make that "ULTIMATE" sacrifice to God, to end the life of His son Issac, would you? Like the widow of Zarephath, would you offer your last meal to a stranger?

FAITH OVER FEAR

How do you "act" faith?

A preacher once said, "give till it hurts, give till you can give no more". The life you save now can yield you unimaginable returns. Have faith – "FAITH" in God daily. This is "Faith in action".

Hebrews 11:1
Now faith is the substance of things hoped for, the evidence of things not seen.

YOU ARE AWESOME

One of a Kind

be happy

Smile More!

BE HOPEFUL

HAVE FAITH

YOU ARE CARING

you are loved

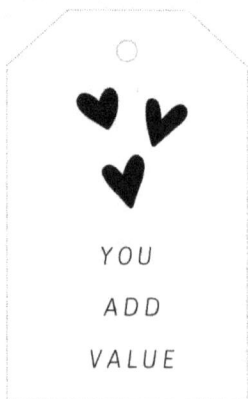

YOU ADD VALUE

4
Prayer and Miracles

Prayer and Miracles.

Prayer Can Move Mountains-We Ought To Believe This.

"If you're not sure about the power of prayer, it is because you don't pray. Prayer has divided the sea. Prayer brought water out of solid rock. Prayer cooled off Nebuchadnezzar's fiery furnace. Prayer blocked the lions' mouths so they couldn't destroy Daniel".
--- Pastor C.D. Brooks. (Adventist Quotes)

When we pray

When we pray and God answers, His response to our supplications seem like magic or miracles to us; but because God is all powerful to do the normal, the usual ,and the extraordinary on our behalf, things that may appear too difficult and unattainable become easy, simple, and ordinary by God's intervention in our lives, because we pray and trust Him honestly, earnestly and with abiding faith.

Exodus 14:21 "And Moses stretched out his hand over the sea; and the Lord caused the sea to go back by a strong east wind all that night, and made the sea become dry land, and the waters were divided".

Exodus 17:5 "Then the Lord told Moses, "Go over in front of the people and take some of the elders of Israel with you. Take in your hand the staff with which you struck the Nile, and go",(verse) 6, I'll be standing there in front of you on the rock at Horeb. You are to strike the rock and water will come out of it, so the people can drink." Moses did this in front of the elders of Israel".

Daniel 3:24-25 Then Nebuchadnezzar, the king, was astonished, and rose up in haste, and spake, and said unto his counselors, "did not we cast three men, bound into the midst of the fire?" They answered and said unto the king, "true, O king."

He answered and said," Lo, I see four men loose, walking in the midst of the fire, and they have no hurt; and the form of the fourth is like the Son of God". Yes, indeed!

Faith can move mountains, part seas. as well as cool a fiery furnace.

Daniel 6:17-20 "A stone was brought and placed over the mouth of the den, and the king sealed it with his own signet ring and with the rings of his nobles, so that Daniel's situation might not be changed. Then the king returned to his palace and spent the night without eating and without any entertainment being brought to him. And he could not sleep".

At the first light of dawn, the king got up and hurried to the lions' den. When he came near the den, he called to Daniel in an anguished voice, "Daniel, servant of the living God, has your God whom you serve continually been able to rescue you from the lions?"

"Yes, INDEED," is the correct answer.

5
Power of Prayer

Power of Prayer

Pray,just pray!

Pray without ceasing in any language you may speak. Our God is still in the business of answering humble prayers of faith. He never fails to answer in the right manner, at the right time, and in clear and powerful ways.

Pray to God as if you are speaking with a friend: be honest and realistic as to your expectations. Nothing is too big nor too small to ask from God. Have faith . Believe that God will answer your prayers according to His manifold blessings- leave the decision to Him as to when and how He answers you. JUST PRAY!

Sometimes, His answer could be YES, sometimes, NO, and sometimes, "WAIT" He always answers!

Power of God

Our faith, belief, humility, and confidence in the power of God to move in our lives, cannot be underestimated. These are very difficult times: we may be incapable of solving our problems or meeting our own needs, but God can. He listens, He cares. He just wants us to ask. Whatever the severity of our challenges, God is always able to attend to our needs.

What He did for the Israelites in their flight from the bondage in Egypt, He still is able to do for us today. Stop and reflect over your own life, "count your many blessings (and) see what God has done", as the song says.

His word says, "Seek and you shall find, knock and it shall be opened unto you". Matthew 7: 7-8 True!

Our job is to trust and call on God in earnest prayer.

"The ball field is vast. Just throw out that pitch, because God has got your bases covered",Yes!!!

Just throw out that pitch in complete faith; you will "score", because God has you covered - with "bases loaded". Just pray, without ceasing and with complete faith in God.

6
Love as God Loves

Love As God Loves

1 John 4:8 He that loveth not knoweth not God; for God is love. (He loves, He cares, He gives- always).

"The love of God is greater far, than pen or tongue can ever tell", so states the song writer, Frederick M Lehman.

You are made in the image of God. Can we love, or are we willing to love like God who made us in His image, and gave His son Jesus Christ to die and save us from our own sins?

Are you willing to Love as your creator God gave and still gives, endlessly!

Try it. It could really defeat our "loving, selfish" desires and acts.

Start now-selflessly, and earnestly caring for others could just work for you.

I firmly believe it would.

May God bless you richly!!!

7
Don't Stay Fallen

No excuses to remain fallen: - setbacks must not fail you.

According to Joe Girard, "the elevator to success is out of order". "You'll have to use the staircase, one step at a time".

Things could get tough along the way: then what? Stay focused!

It could get worse when the steps lose their interconnected integrity, and you have nothing to elevate yourself to your intended destination. "Make hay" now while it is day and "the sun (still) shines".

Darkness is just ahead when your vision, as in choices, would surely become limited. Stop wishing for the golden parachute, or this and that...! Do something good with what's available to you until something better happens for you.

Make it a great day!!! (Oh wait: - God bless you)!

So, do you just throw your hands up and hang your feet up in the air and just give up? You can't! Even if you foolishly decide to do the latter, the all constant gravitational force will not allow you. You will surely fall or just crash, like "Humpty Dumpty", into pieces, such that you may never be put together again. No amount of crazy glue can then put you together again- figuratively speaking.

Never give up on your dreams or aspirations because of a few hiccups on the way. As they say, "pick yourself up by your bootstraps" and keep climbing "upwards". It is true that there are many negative forces that would look to pulling you down at all cost, but there are usually many more that are looking to helping you rise above your difficulties.

I was terrified of going to New York city because it is supposed to be a really rough place. Then a young pastor told me not to be so afraid because while what I already heard may be true, there are lots more good people than the "bad apples" in and around the "big apple", New York city, (Lol).

As a famous empathetic and realistic American would say, it does not matter how many times you fall, "ya keep gettin' up", and I may add, keep rising up till you can stand on your once rubbery legs, and walk, even, run: okay, don't get carried way now- don't try to fly- "you ain't got no wings", be realistic!

Good luck. "God love ya"!

THINK positive

8
The Gold in Humans

The "Gold" in Humans.

Prov 11:27
Anyone can find the dirt in someone else, but you can be the one who finds the gold.
Your Lord and Savior Jesus Christ did. He found a bunch of lowly placed "fish hunters" and He made them real "fishers of men". From these people, we now have the gospels and Judaeo-Christian teachings that most of us adhere to today.

How often do we see people and declare how inadequate, how dirty,and how undesirable, they appear in our eyes and minds! (You'll see)!!!

Take a moment, take a few steps backwards and recognize the goodness that others possess, and give thanks to our Creator for the good in these other people. Just take a few moments!

Someone once told me in a conversation that God must really have a great sense of humor-the same God who made the peacock and other beautiful creatures also made the ugly hippopotamus, the elephants, and the Rhinos – strange looking animals, some would say, but look how much the ivory from the previous two are so desired that human beings kill them for their expensive tusks.

Can you imagine how rich (to farmers) the dung from hippos and elephants could be!

The news has it that the Chinese and other Asian countries are importing cow dung from India for their farming needs. "Go figure"!

Let's talk about schools: Elementary, Secondary, Universities, (technical Schools- included), together can constitute the great equalizer in learning. Every faculty attracts a different crowd of learners.

Many of them become experts in those disciplines and skills. Those who love the Arts may hate Science and Engineering, but each must appreciate the other. There are the professions: Law, Engineering, and Medicine – all have something to offer. How can I omit the construction workers and laborers! Without these, the work- of the Engineers and Architects could just be paper tigers, full of wise directives, but lacking in implementation by those skilled in carrying out those directives; think about it!

Have you ever encountered people picking up garbage from your streets? They are important too and we ought to appreciate them as we appreciate ourselves and our own professions. Everyone is important, everyone matters and ought to be valued.

A preacher once declared that Jesus kept bad company. He went on to explain:

Peter- He was liar. Three times he denied knowing Jesus Christ.

Judas Iscariot – He was a traitor- he betrayed his Lord and sold Jesus Christ for thirty pieces of "talents" . He later found his loot useless, and tried his best to return that "blood money", but it was too late- nobody wanted to have anything to do with that income derived from treachery.

Rehab (the harlot) – She was one of the ancestors of Jesus Christ.

King David: - He was also in the lineage of our Savior Jesus Christ, but he was covetous, a liar,an adulterer, and a murderer, but he was declared to be a man after God's heart. Yes, don't forget he gave us Psalm 23; "The Lord is my shepherd…" Think about that!

There is a lot more.

The truth of the matter is that Jesus Christ never became like these people were. He did not mire himself in their short falls or sins. He showed them a better way, then He gave His life to save all: all that would believe in Him!

At crucifixion, he was flanked by two thieves, still bad company, even unto death. He died to save them too, though only one accepted that salvation. "C'est la vie". (That's the world we live in).

Would you do something great for another life today just for the sake of it, without expecting any reward! There is inherently something good in every human being.We need to believe this, or at least, try to.

Always remember, man/woman was part of the creation of God that He Himself pronounced "good".

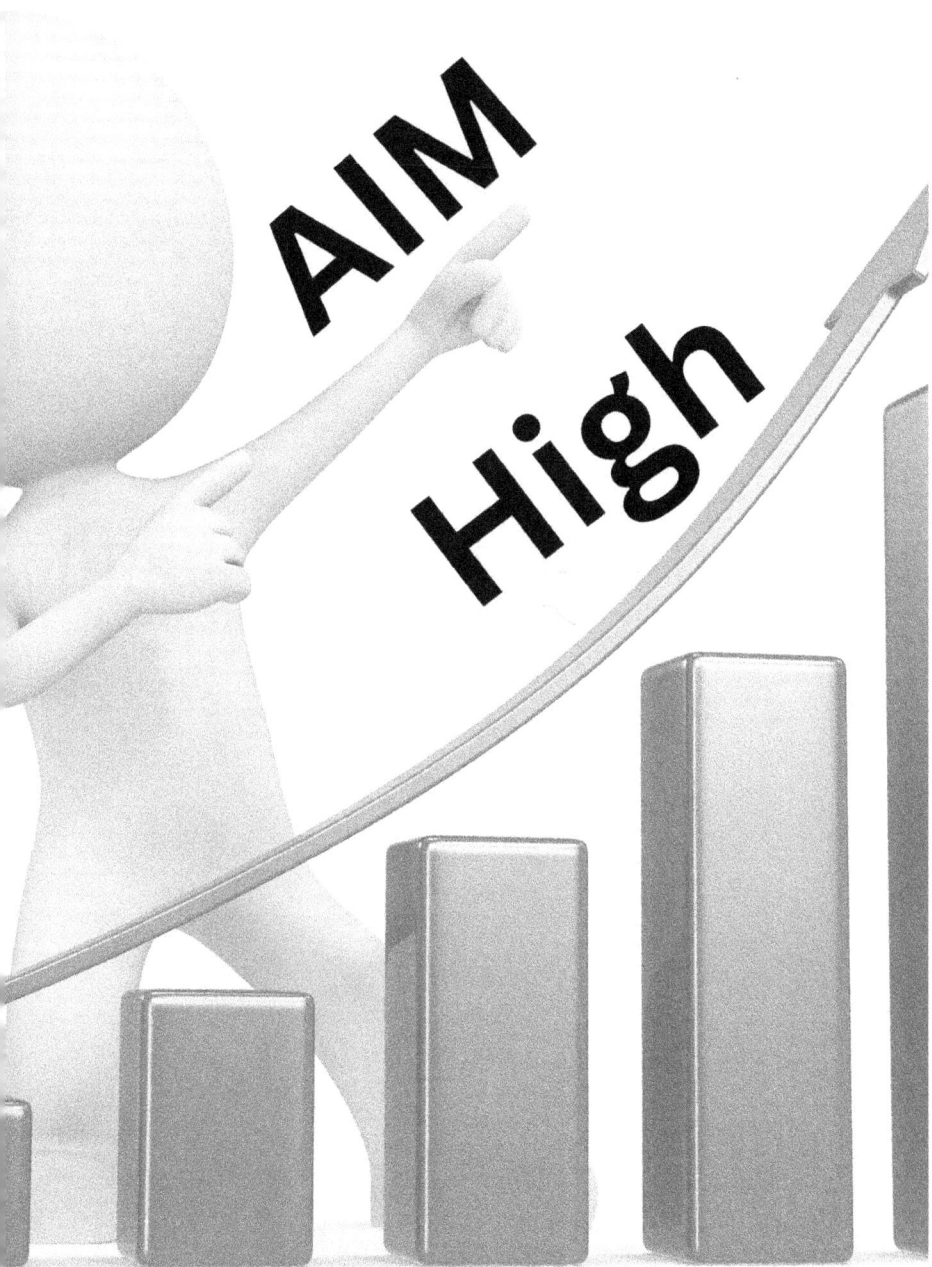

9
Action Compliments Faith

Action Compliments Faith.

Faith does not make things easy; it makes them possible. "For with God, nothing shall be impossible". (Luke 1:37)

Just proclaiming faith is not enough for the endless possibilities that result from true faith, for "faith without works is dead".

What does it profit us as human beings if we say that we have faith but do nothing about it? Can faith alone save man?" (James 2:14)." For as the body without the spirit is dead, so faith without works is dead also" (James 2:26).

As an old preacher once said, "have faith, but do something until something happens".
Pray!

If we ask God, we must believe that He will answer. We must do our share too. We must "Act"!

Ask Me Anything

God Will Answer

10
The Bane of Self

"Me, Myself and I", for Others, and with Others.

Two men went "fishing". They worked hard and were richly blessed. One of the two shared some of his wealth, helping to uplift and pave the way to success in the lives of the young and needy. One taught all of us valuable lessons in selflessness and hope. The other, he exercised his right to self and selfishness.

He picked up a flashy, expensive, and fast depreciating toy. Within minutes, there was a crash and his priced toy got massively mangled and lost value instantly. He was also badly hurt, but survived.

On the other hand, some of the recipients of the benevolence of the considerate guy left college without debts and went on to help others in like manner, eschewing selfishness and promoting selfless living for others.

Yes, the selfless man promoted hope, progress and prosperity, while the self centered man spent and lived lavishly, only for a time. He harvested pain and suffering in the process. He did not leave a legacy of goodness nor hope for others.

If you keep up with the news, you know who they are. This is a true story, without naming names. Who are they? Your comment, please!

No one should envy those who are rich, especially if they have earned their wealth. No one should!

For those who want to be team players, (and we all should be), there is, indeed, "no I" in the word team. I certainly agree. Do you?

The question is, "Do you consider your wealth something you can thank God for and maybe consider a little bit of your "overflow" to help society to ameliorate the pain of suffering or do you feel you should keep

the whole "shabbang" and spend as selfishly as you "darn well please", or do you share a little of it with others! Think about it! If you have remained in the true, "myself, and I" selfish camp, consider decamping now.

Lighten the load for others and for "good"- that will be the right thing to do, and you could be a much happier person for doing so.

Here is the question: are you willing to give to those in need without expecting any personal rewards, are you?

11
Team

Team.

" Alone I can "speak", but together we can talk". Alone, I can enjoy, but together we can celebrate. "Alone, I can smile, but together, we can laugh." Here then is the beauty of Human Relations.
From "Good morning"

"Coach, there is no 'I' in team". Other people have stated that "I" is in center of the word "sin".
"Cooperation is a good word", a musician once wrote. All things being equal, teamwork and cooperation will lead to the achievement of goals: together!

A teenager in a soccer team, after a very important meeting with his coach and team members, looked at the coach and said, "couch, there is no 'I' in team" (He meant coach, not couch- he was a high school fresh man, ninth grader).

The correct spelling is very important, but the "thought counts".

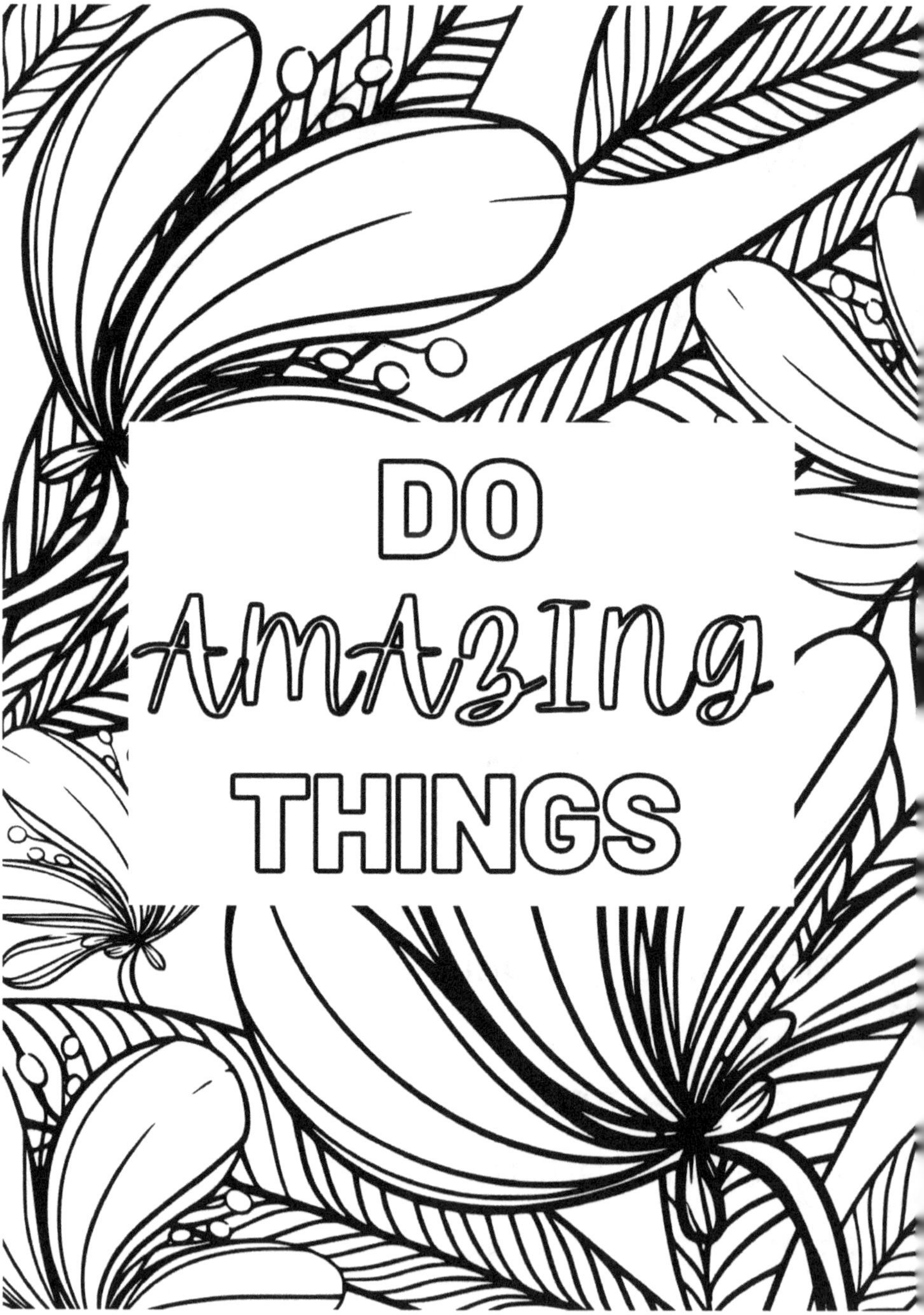
DO
AMAZING
THINGS

12
I Can't

"I CAN'/t"

"if you are serious about achieving Success in any area of your life, you must master your mindset".
(Thomas Oppong)

If you think you can, you probably will succeed in your endeavor. If you feel you may not succeed, you will probably fail.
Change your "I can't" to "I can"! "Yes, you can".

A good secret to success is a positive mindset.

YOU CAN DO IT

If you fail, never give up because F.A.I.L stands for
 " First Attempt in Learning", they say.

End is not the end, in fact E.N.D stands for
"Effort Never Dies", it is said.

If you get "No" for an answer, remember "no" stands for
 " Next Opportunity"- yet another saying.

So, lets get moving towards success until we achieve and never give up.

you Can Be
WHATEVER
YOU WANT

13
Just Think

Just Think.

Be Warned, Be Sensible.

"He who gets run over by a heavy, noisy locomotive engine or train, was not killed by the train, but died only from the deafness of his own ears and the blindness of his own eyes". (-West African proverb)

You should have seen and heard that big and noisy locomotive approaching and done the right thing- "get out of the way". You cannot "kill" a big, bad, moving, noisy, heavy locomotive; it would be senseless, infact insane.

You cannot stand against a heavy, fast moving locomotive, even if you are firing an AK-47 rifle at it. It would not work against that "beast" or any engine. Get out of the way and live to fight another day.

A word to the wise-think and stay safe!

Sometimes we hear and see danger coming our way and refuse to get out of the way- well, you know the sad ending. You may not be run over by some mechanical, moving, "big guy", but for now, we must listen to the experts and take advice and precautions to avoid being decimated by this pandemic, this dreaded Covid -19. "A word to the wise..."

Wash those hands and Mask up.

14
It is All About You

It is All About You

"The biggest source of motivation are your own thoughts. So, think big and motivate yourself to win."
(From "Always Positive").

Yes, it's all about you – "The hardest battle you will ever have to fight is between who you are now and who you want to be in the future.

I hope you choose a better future for who you want to be. The power is in you to choose right!
(From" Pure Happy Life").

Many of us usually complain about how bad things have been for us in general. We continue in the path of doing the same things we had done in the past and continuously getting the same results we do not like.

Fight the battle: Change who you are now so you can become who you want to be. Let go of your negative attitude towards others, life itself, and in fact, yourself.

Motivate yourself to wake up a few minutes early every day, maybe spend a little time in prayer and meditation.

You could do a few things you don't normally do, like tidying up, one desk, maybe one room at a time.

Say less hurtful words to your family and friends and more encouraging words to people in general, and everyday. Just try it! Increase useful activities in your life. Get more active productively.

It Starts With You

Don't be lazy, take responsibility for your actions. When you do, this action alone has a funny way of helping you to do better next time for yourself as well as for others. Before you know it, you would have formed the habit of motivating yourself, as well as others, to be a lot better, happier and successful person than you were yesterday.

Do you believe in the power of prayer? Try it fervently. It could just make your journey smoother, even if "it is not an easy road".

Good luck and may God bless you and "keep you" on a better path and state than that in which you were yesterday, or are at the moment for that matter.

15
Empathy

Empathy

"He who just swallows does not understand the grinding that he who must chew first before swallowing must go through": –a translation of an old West African adage.

Empathy goes a long way to understanding and appreciating your "neighbor". An old American Indian proverb states, "before you blame the Indian, walk a mile in his moccasins". We must take heed to this advice.

Let's cultivate it in our daily lives. May God bless us as He always does, but may we be humble and ready to share those blessings that we so freely and frequently receive from God our heavenly Father.

"Matthew 10:8 Freely ye have received, freely give"!

Be Thankful
Be Grateful
Be Blessed

DREAM BIG

Scriptural Quotes to "Ponder".

Scriptural Quotes
to "Ponder".

Isaiah 41:10
"Fear not, for I am with you;
Be not dismayed, for I am your God.
I will strengthen you,
Yes, I will help you,
I will uphold you with My righteous right
hand".

Romans 8:28
"And we know that all things work together
for good to those who love God, to those
who are the called according to His
purpose".

Romans 15:13
"Now may the God of hope fill you with all
joy and peace in believing, that you may
abound in hope by the power of the Holy
Spirit".

Philippians 4:6
"Be anxious for nothing, but in everything by prayer and supplication, with thanksgiving, let your requests be made known to God".

Hebrews 13:6
So we may boldly say:
"The LORD is my helper;
I will not fear.
What can man do to me?"

Ephesians 4:31
"Let all bitterness, wrath, anger, [a]clamor, and evil speaking be put away from you, with all malice".

Ephesians 6:10-11
"Finally, my brethren, be strong in the Lord and in the power of His might. 11 Put on the whole armor of God, that you may be able to stand against the [a]wiles of the devil".

Ephesians 4:32
"And be kind to one another, tenderhearted, forgiving one another, even as God in Christ forgave you".

Psalm 28:7
"The LORD is my strength and my shield;
My heart trusted in Him, and I am helped;
Therefore my heart greatly rejoices,
And with my song I will praise Him".

1 Corinthians 13:4-7
4 "Love suffers long and is kind; love does not envy; love does not parade itself, is not puffed up; 5 does not behave rudely, does not seek its own, is not provoked, thinks no evil; 6 does not rejoice in iniquity, but rejoices in the truth; 7 bears all things, believes all things, hopes all things, endures all things".

1 Peter 5:7
"Cast all your anxiety on him because he cares for you".

Psalm 46:1
"God is our refuge and strength, an ever-present help in trouble".

Isaiah 41:10
"So do not fear, for I am with you;do not be dismayed, for I am your God.
I will strengthen you and help you; I will uphold you with my righteous right hand".

Joshua 1:9
"Have I not commanded you? Be strong and courageous. Do not be afraid; do not be discouraged, for the Lord your God will be with you wherever you go."

Psalm 94:18-19

18 "When I said, "My foot is slipping,"
   your unfailing love, Lord, supported
me.
19 When anxiety was great within me,
   your consolation brought me joy".

2 Timothy 1:7
"For the Spirit God gave us does not
make us timid, but gives us power, love
and self-discipline".

Matthew 11:28
 "Come to me, all you who are weary
and burdened, and I will give you rest".

1 Thessalonians 5:11
"Therefore encourage one another and
build each other up, just as in fact you
are doing".

17
Prayer

A psalm of David. Psalm 23

1
The Lord is my shepherd, I lack nothing.
2
   He makes me lie down in green pastures,
he leads me beside quiet waters,
3
   he refreshes my soul.
He guides me along the right paths
   for his name's sake.
4
Even though I walk
   through the darkest valley,[a]
I will fear no evil,
   for you are with me;
your rod and your staff,
   they comfort me.

5
You prepare a table before me
   in the presence of my enemies.
You anoint my head with oil;
   my cup overflows.
6
Surely your goodness and love will follow me
   all the days of my life,
and I will dwell in the house of the Lord
   forever.

Psalm 121
A song of ascents.

1
I lift up my eyes to the mountains—
   where does my help come from?
2
My help comes from the Lord,
   the Maker of heaven and earth.

3
He will not let your foot slip—
   he who watches over you will not slumber;
4
indeed, he who watches over Israel
   will neither slumber nor sleep.

5
The Lord watches over you—
   the Lord is your shade at your right hand;
6
the sun will not harm you by day,
   nor the moon by night.

7
The Lord will keep you from all harm—
   he will watch over your life;
8
the Lord will watch over your coming and going
   both now and forevermore.

Psalm 27

1 The Lord is my light and my salvation—
    whom shall I fear?
The Lord is the stronghold of my life—
    of whom shall I be afraid?

2 When the wicked advance against me
    to devour[a] me,
it is my enemies and my foes
    who will stumble and fall.
3 Though an army besiege me,
    my heart will not fear;
though war break out against me,
    even then I will be confident.

4 One thing I ask from the Lord,
    this only do I seek:
that I may dwell in the house of the Lord
    all the days of my life,
to gaze on the beauty of the Lord
    and to seek him in his temple.
5 For in the day of trouble
    he will keep me safe in his dwelling;
he will hide me in the shelter of his sacred tent
    and set me high upon a rock.

6 Then my head will be exalted
    above the enemies who surround me;
at his sacred tent I will sacrifice with shouts of joy;
    I will sing and make music to the Lord.

7 Hear my voice when I call, Lord;
  be merciful to me and answer me.
8 My heart says of you, "Seek his face!"
  Your face, Lord, I will seek.
9 Do not hide your face from me,
  do not turn your servant away in anger;
  you have been my helper.
Do not reject me or forsake me,
  God my Savior.

10
Though my father and mother forsake me,
  the Lord will receive me.
11
Teach me your way, Lord;
  lead me in a straight path
  because of my oppressors.
12
Do not turn me over to the desire of my foes,
  for false witnesses rise up against me,
  spouting malicious accusations.

13
I remain confident of this:
  I will see the goodness of the Lord
  in the land of the living.
14
Wait for the Lord;
  be strong and take heart
  and wait for the Lord.